AmericanGirl Library®

True Stories

Girls' inspiring stories of courage and heart

AmericanGirl®

Questions or comments? Call 1-800-845-0005,
or write American Girl, P.O. Box 620497, Middleton, WI 53562-0497.

Visit our Web site at americangirl.com.

Printed in China
05 06 07 08 09 LEO 10 9 8 7 6 5 4

American Girl® and American Girl Library® are registered trademarks
of American Girl, LLC.

Editorial Development: Trula Magruder, Shannon Payette, Michelle Watkins

Art Direction and Design: Chris David and Camela Decaire

Production: Kendra Pulvermacher, Mindy Rappe, Jeannette Bailey, Judith Lary

Illustrations: Amanda Haley

Cover Photography: Jamie Young

Dear Reader,

For years, girls have loved True Stories in American Girl magazine. The stories make you laugh—and sometimes cry. But mostly, they make you say, "Wow! That's amazing!"

In this collection, you'll hear from girls who've had experiences that tapped strength, compassion, creativity, and courage they didn't know they had inside. Imagine:

- You get a letter from a pen pal who's nothing like you. Do you write back?

- You want to help kids in the hospital feel better, but how?

- Your bus driver suddenly faints while driving you to school. How would you react?

The girls who wrote these stories hoped to inspire girls like you to make a difference in your community, to be strong when faced with a challenge, and to know that when really hard times hit, there will always be other girls out there who know what you're going through.

Is there a true story bubbling inside you? Whether it's an exciting story or just an ordinary problem, your story matters. Tell it.

Your friends at American Girl

Contents

Giving Back

Disaster

Friends

Rescues

Obstacles

Heroes

how I ...
same time. I us...
and cry when I s...
    On Decembe...
golden brown pupp...
thought she was pi...
come outside to see...
EVERYTHING we co...
later, our neighbors s...
dog lived a block away...
was neglected and left...
would see her out side ...
owners fed her disgu...
brother (Matth...
when she ...
much

Dear American Girl Mag...

I love your magazine and I like...
magazine. I have been waiting for a cha...
happened to me in my life. This week...
following story is about my cousins...
to us. I would be so excited if th...
could try to fit it into one of y...
obliged. So enough talk, n...
cousins that live in Long ...

This summer I we...
expecting it to...
walks, and ...
bored by ...
have a ...
ove...
b...

c...
wh...
I'...
broth...
lear...

Dear American Girl,

    I was vacationing...
our summer ham...
with my dad on h...
—to go moose h...
—up on a mou...
when I ...
A ma...
lo...

Dear American
    I'm hoping
put my true sto
magazine. 'Cause =
it touched people
everywhere aroun
world. Here Goes!
    The day wa
31, 1997, and I was
my ninth birthday in
place with some of
very

we...
pan...
tl...
and ...
party
invitation
to call n
wouldn't s
talked with n
they could
d party good
ts of waiting,
a story to
catering hall get ... day came. ...
... and then
... after the ...
my parents ...

SURPRISE !!

nto were so surprised to s...
do and family. They near...
as so much fun. She...
selves a lot. ...

her name
on August 21,
he lives alone in
of her gard
he was
7 a

my family
on the wa
happened

e ient a
kids involve
also adults
playing
and

True S
American Girl
This is a true st
rga
ono
uck
Mor
9,

t vo
n you
now
eart
h

Dear American Girl,
   Here is my true story.

      In May, I got to do something r
officer all day. The local Optimists C'
day where older Girl Scouts pair tog
to see what their day is like. I first n
was paired with at a breakfast in a
day. We h

Dear America
You hear stor
send messages in b
one about
ched to ba
nk so. I, or
message ac
alloon. I
rrington, I
a place
arolin
4 d
er

Giving Back

True Story

Dear American Girl,
I have proof that birthday wishes really do come true!
   On my thirteenth birthday   I made a wish and
         ow out the candles. My   Tennessee
                y best friend,   nett,

Dear American Girl,
r American Girl

A Cut Above

Kelli opens her heart with locks of love.

Finally, the big day arrived for my sister and me to cut our hair for Locks of Love. Our donated hair would be used to make wigs for kids who can't grow hair because of medical conditions. Michelle got her hair cut first by our sister Elisa, who was crying and shaking so hard, she could hardly cut

Michelle's ponytail. Michelle started crying, and then I did. I was taking pictures of the big event and could hardly see through the viewfinder.

When it was my turn, I was really nervous, so Michelle took me to a salon. Tears spilled from my eyes when I heard the first snip of the scissors. I couldn't believe that I had actually cut off my long hair! When we got out to the car, I just sat there and cried. I felt like I was

truly giving of myself. I was giving someone a part of me, giving something that meant a lot to me. I was sad to lose my hair but happy someone else would benefit from it.

My mom had cut off ten inches of her hair in college and hadn't thrown it away. It was just enough to send to Locks of Love, too. It was cool that my mom supported us and that the three of us were in on this together.

I was worried most about what people would think when I went back to school after Christmas break, but a lot of people didn't even notice my short hair! My close friends did, of course. One friend even said she was going to donate her hair after I told her why I had cut mine. That made me feel good.

I am used to having short hair now. When people ask me why I cut it, I only have to tell them about Locks of Love.

Kelli K.

Age 13, Utah

Kelli, left, with her sister Michelle, before and after their haircuts. To find out more about donating, go to *locksoflove.org*.

The Greatest Gift

An act of kindness changes Vanessa's life.

I used to have long brown curly hair. I really liked it and people always told me it was beautiful. When I was two, I developed alopecia areata (that means I was "allergic" to my hair and it would fall out) and eczema. When the condition first appeared, I lost most of my hair, but it grew back. Over the years, patches would fall out, but I was always able to cover them.

When I was 9, the doctors told my parents we needed to move from the California desert because the climate was drying out my skin. Right before we moved, my hair started to fall out again.

After we moved, I was nervous about starting fourth grade at a new school. By now, I was completely bald. I bought a wig made of fake hair, but it was itchy and didn't stay on. Every time I tried to play, it would turn sideways and embarrass me.

I decided to wear a bandanna when I started school. I made nice friends, but I was asked a lot of questions and was made fun of at times. Sometimes, I would just sit and cry really hard.

When I would come home after a tough day, Mom would say if people don't accept me, then they have the problem, not me. She would kiss my head and tell me how she loves me without hair, because hair hid my beautiful face.

I asked Mom why this had happened to me and not to one of my sisters or brother. Why couldn't I have been normal? Mom told me that most people aren't normal. Everyone has challenges in life—some people get sick, some are sad, some lose their jobs. Sometimes bad things happen to people when they're young and sometimes when they're old. She said maybe God had given me these problems so that I could grow up to help other kids. She made me feel a lot better.

And then an act of kindness changed my life. I got a hairpiece from Locks of Love. The wig, made of real human hair donated by adults and kids, seals to your head like a suction cup. I was so happy when the wig came. It was really long and the same color of hair I used to have. It was so beautiful that after my mom put it on me, I ran outside, jumped up and down, and turned somersaults. I tried everything in my wig and it wouldn't fall off!

I felt much better when I went out. Nobody stared at me anymore! Lots of people even told me I had beautiful hair.

These disorders have made me a different person. I am always aware if someone is sad, is made fun of, or is stared at. I always make friends with kids new in school or kids who get teased. I am stronger and a little bit older inside because of all I have been through.

I wonder if people who donate to Locks of Love know how much they help kids. Do they realize how much they are changing someone else's life for the better? I know how important hair is. The people who donate theirs must be especially nice.

Vanessa
Age 11, Virginia

Fur Love

Maeghan and Spice make a hospital nice.

I started going to hospitals when I was eight years old. I wasn't sick. I had a medicine doctors couldn't offer—my lovable golden retriever!

Maeghan gives Spice and Ben a little of her own love therapy.

A therapy dog goes to nursing homes and hospitals to visit the sick or elderly. The dog learns to be obedient, comfortable around wheelchairs or walkers, and careful around medical equipment. Dogs shouldn't step on the air tubes of people on oxygen! Spice and I had to be tested and observed to see how she would react to different situations. When I was 12, my dog Spice and I became a therapy team.

One person Spice and I always like to visit is Doris. Doris has a disease that affects her nervous and muscular systems. When we first met Doris, she was in a wheelchair. She couldn't get up alone or dress herself, and she was getting stiffer and stiffer.

In the beginning, Doris had a tough time petting Spice. She worked hard at using her arms and hands to accomplish this feat. Our visits were like physical

therapy. Doris would pet Spice and talk to her about her life. She told Spice all about the dogs she'd had when she was a little girl. I could see Doris remembering those days with each stroke of Spice's fur. The visits seemed to take her mind off her problems and her disease. She looked forward to seeing us.

Doris has been improving a lot these days. Now when Spice and I visit, we see her strolling the halls with her walker! It's fulfilling to know that we can make people feel happiness and joy, even if it's for a few minutes or a few strokes of fur.

Maeghan B.

Age 15, Virginia

14

Video Star

Megan's video drive earns two thumbs up!

I was born with a condition called hemifacial dysplasia. It is what I have, but it is not who I am. The condition has caused me to be blind in one eye and to need lots of surgeries. I have had 19 operations so far, and I will need many more in the future.

When I was younger, I was happy just to have my mom hold me the whole time I was in the hospital. But as I got older and spent more time in hospitals, I got bored quickly and wanted something to do to pass the time. Usually there wasn't anything on TV, and the few videos available for kids my age were always checked out.

One day, I told my mom that I wanted to collect enough videos to give to both of the children's hospitals in our area. So I asked my Girl Scout troop to help. The girls were eager to get involved.

I decided to call the project "Kids Helping Kids." We contacted local television stations and talked to the local newspapers. I also asked other Girl Scout troops in the area to help. Several troops put collection bins in their schools. My troop put bins in local grocery stores.

Kids
Helping
Kids

Whenever a TV station ran our story, the bins were filled that day. It was amazing! Each time I unloaded videos from one of those bins, I knew that hospitalized kids were going to be so happy! One of the reporters asked me how many videos I had hoped to collect. I told him 500. I thought my mom would faint when she learned that we ended up collecting more than 1,500 videos!

We collected enough videos to donate quite a few to five children's hospitals in Washington and Oregon. They were the kind of videos that kids really want to watch, like "Matilda," Disney classics, and "Spy Kids." People are so kind and caring when it comes to helping kids in need.

I am now trying to get Girl Scout troops all across the United States to participate in the "Kids Helping Kids" video drive. I want them to collect videos for the children's hospital closest to them. I have troops in some states that have already told me they would love to do this project, but I won't quit until I have at least one troop in every state.

My video drive didn't save a life or change the world. But I know from experience that if one child lying in the hospital is a little happier because of this, then it was worth every minute I put into it.

Megan J.
Age 10, Washington

Can-Do Spirit
Devon dares to dream big.

Devon surrounded by some of her recyclables

I started recycling cans as a way to learn to manage my money. My parents encouraged me to take a quarter of the earnings to the grocery store, buy a can of cat food, and take it to the local Humane Society. It made me feel so good, I wanted to save even more money so that I could donate more often.

One day, a neighbor gave me a large bag of aluminum cans. I cashed in the cans at a local recycling plant. It felt so fulfilling, I wanted to recycle lots more.

I collected cans from neighbors and picked up cans along the side of the road. As I talked to different people about what I was doing, a few businesses asked me to pick up their recyclable materials. I discovered that I could really make a difference. Local businesses didn't get recycling services, so somebody at work would have to take the recyclables home, or they would have to go to a landfill.

Before long I had my own business. I got more customers. It wasn't tough going into offices—I really believed in what I was doing! After all, who would say no to having a free collection service and helping the environment at the same time? Today I recycle about 7,000 cans a month from more than 80 businesses!

I call my business "Devon's Heal the World." What started as a way to make money now has a higher cause—to help protect the environment. I look forward to the day when there is a branch of Heal the World in every neighborhood, every state, and every nation.

Most people tell me that they are amazed about what I am doing at such an early age. I believe one person—even a young person—can make a difference. Setting an example and cleaning up a neighborhood can lead other kids to do something similar themselves.

If you really want to make a difference, you can find a way.

Devon D.

Age 12, Florida

August 21, 1
She lives alone in
of her gard
she was

on the wa
happened

True S
American Girl
This is a true st

organ
Hono
duck
Mor

Dear American Girl,
Here is my true story.

In May, I got to do something r
officer all day. The local Optimists Ch
day where older Girl Scouts pair tog
to see what their day is like. I first r
was paired with at a breakfast in a
day. We ha

Dear Americ
You hear sto
send messages in s
one abo
ched to I
ink so. I
message
Balloon, c
rrington,
a place
arolin
4 d

AMISH QUILT 34 USA

Disaster

True Story

Dear American Girl,
I have proof that birthday wishes really do come true!
On my thirteenth birthday   Tennessee
blew out the candles. My
best friend,
nett.

Dear American Girl,

Twister!

A tornado puts Sydney's life in a spin.

I was watching a movie with my mom and brothers on a humid and cloudy day in June. Dad was out of town. The clouds started to get really dark, so I let the dog in. Before long, it started raining and hail pounded on our roof.

Suddenly we heard a loud clap of thunder, and our television went out. The clouds looked threatening and hail grew to the size of softballs! We moved into the laundry room, where it was safer.

Even though I could see trees falling down outside, everything was quiet. Then my mom whispered words I never thought I'd hear: "Oh my God, this is a tornado."

Before I could think about what Mom had just said, I heard the sound of a train running over us—and then our roof blew off! Mom tried to shield us with her arm, but roofing, dust, and household items blew all over us. I thought we were going to die. I thought the tornado was going to pick us up and kill us.

Only a minute later, the noise was gone. We walked out of the laundry room and saw broken glass all over the house.

All five members of my family had to sleep in the same bed in our house that night. The house was too damaged to stay in any longer. The next day we drove to St. Paul, Minnesota, where my dad works, and for the next month, we camped out at different hotels.

When we finally returned home, we could use only one room. It was cramped and smelled moldy. The tornado had blown out all of our windows, so whenever it rained, water would get in. We had to wear shoes all the time because of all the broken glass. It was horrible!

The shock of the tornado still haunts me. I'm learning to cope with the fear of severe weather. But I've realized that no matter how bad things get, I can always find the good in life. My family made it through safely, and that is all that matters.

Age 12, Wisconsin

High-Water Hardships
Flood chores leave Casey drained.

We left Disney World after my grandmother called to tell us that a tropical storm was expected to flood our neighborhood. As soon as we got home, we saw our field filled with disgusting, coffee-colored water.

With the water so high, Casey's house looks like a houseboat!

But it didn't stop there. The next morning, the water rose as high as my horses' heads and surrounded our home. Ants were everywhere, and my dad fell and broke his ankle while trying to spray them. That made life even worse, because he couldn't help us with a lot of the work that needed to be done.

When we went to or from school or anywhere else, we had to paddle a boat or walk in deep water. I had to

help paddle and got frustrated because it made my arms tired, and I kept getting wet trying to get in and out of the boat.

While the water continued to rise outside, inside we didn't have a drop. With no running water in the house for nearly two weeks, we had to paddle to Aunt Martie's for a bath.

My day went like this: Get up, brush my teeth with bottled water, put on play clothes, get in the boat, paddle to the end of the street, tie up the boat, get in our truck, and change into school clothes. After school, my aunt would drive us to her house to take a bath and get ready for bed. Later, my mom would pick us up. We would load bottled water from the Red Cross onto the boat and paddle back home. It was exhausting!

The flood was the worst two weeks that I have ever had to live through and something I will always remember. It was tough, and at times we got angry with each other, but we quickly learned to work together as a family. And I think we all felt that through it all, things were really O.K. because we had each other.

Casey W.

Age 11, Florida

Casey with her feet on dry land!

Raging Wildfire

Heat and smoke force Bailey from her home.

I live on a ranch that's been in our family for 80 years. Last summer, we thought we might lose it forever.

We'd been at the county fair all week. When we got back, fire trucks were at our gate! The sky was glowing bright orange, and ashes were falling everywhere. The firemen said we had just one hour to pack up and leave.

The fire gets closer to Bailey's home.

When you're deciding what are the most important things to you, an hour goes by really fast. I took my drawings from kindergarten, pictures of my grandparents, and other things I couldn't replace.

The air outside was so hot, it hurt my lungs. We couldn't take all our horses, cows, and chickens with us, so we opened the gates and let them run. We didn't want them to be trapped by the fire. Then we left for town and hoped for the best.

Luckily, the firefighters saved our ranch. A week later, we returned. The mountain was black, and the ashes looked like snow. We rode on horseback for days, looking for our horses and cattle. We found  most of them, except for a calf we'd raised. Some of the cows had burned hooves.

Now the grass is green again, and the deer and elk have returned. I wish the fire had never happened, but I'm glad we're O.K.

Bailey O.

Age 9, Wyoming

Snowbound

Donna gets caught in a sleepover—at Arby's!

We had a sudden snowstorm in my hometown. It started snowing before we left school. As we were getting on the bus, some of the kids said they hoped we would get stuck. Just a few blocks from school, they got their wish.

There was so much snow that the tow trucks couldn't come. Because we had no heat on the bus, our driver walked to an Arby's to see if we could keep warm there. The people not only let us come inside— they gave us all the chicken nuggets, french fries, and soda we wanted!

With more than two feet of snow outside, we couldn't go anywhere. We ended up having to sleep inside the restaurant! People nearby came with blankets and games for us. Some kids slept in booths, and others slept on the floor.

At 3:30 the next morning, my mom came for my brother and me. It had taken her four hours to drive ten blocks! Staying at Arby's was fun, but the best part was not having school for the next two days!

Donna U.

Age 13, New York

Shocking Story

A bolt of lightning gives Sabrina a brainstorm.

My parents and I were hiking in the Grand Canyon when it started to rain. The path uphill was slippery, so we held hands on our way back to the car. Then WHAMMO! Lightning hit us! It was like that tingling feeling you get when your foot goes to sleep, only it went through my whole body. The pain lasted about 45 minutes.

After that, every time there was a thunderstorm, I'd get so scared I'd hide under blankets. Then I started learning about lightning. I even made a Web site so that other kids could learn about lightning, too.

Knowing the facts helped. For instance, you can tell how far away lightning is by counting the seconds between the flash and the thunder. Every five seconds equals one mile. So if you count less than 15 seconds, you're in a high danger zone! Don't take any chances—if you see lightning, or hear thunder, get inside quick!

Sabrina

Age 12, Arizona

27

Bear with Me!
Wild animal feasts from Katie's fridge.

I once lived by a state park on Lake Tahoe in California. One day, my family had just come home from a day trip up north. It was getting dark when we pulled up to our house. My mom noticed that the front door was open, and she asked someone to go turn on the light. My cousin went in and then came out screaming, "There's a bear in the house!"

We didn't know what to do, so we went to the fire station to see if someone could call the sheriff. Then we waited some more. Finally, after an hour, the bear left.

He hadn't broken anything, but the bear somehow had opened our fridge and had eaten all of our food. When we checked the answering machine, the man from the fire station had called. My mom thinks his voice scared the bear out!

Katie D.
Age 12, California

August 21, 1
She lives alone in
of her gar
he was r
g a

on the wa
happened

also involv
playing
and
th

True S
American Gir
This is a true st
orga
ono
duck
Mor

Dear American Girl,
    Here is my true story.

    In May, I got to do something r
officer all day. The local Optimists C
day where older Girl Scouts pair tog
to see what their day is like. I first r
was paired with at a breakfast in a
day. We h

Dear Americe
You hear sto
send messages in l
one abou
ched to l
ink so. I,
message a
balloon.
rrington,
a place
carolir
4 d

Teddy Bears USA 37

Friends

Dear American Girl,
    I have proof that birthday wishes really do come true!
On my thirteenth birthday I made a wish and
w out the candles. My best friend, Tennessee
nett,

Dear American Girl,

True Story

Dear American Girl, **29**

A Perfect Pen Pal
Katie connects with her total opposite.

When my preteen years were beginning, things were not going my way. My best friend and I were giving each other the silent treatment, and my family was as dysfunctional as it could get. I wasn't happy, so I decided to sign up for a pen-pal program.

A few weeks after sending a letter, I got a reply from a girl named Shanna. She seemed to be my total opposite—she was homeschooled, very religious, and not as outgoing as my other friends. Disappointed, I still wrote back, telling Shanna the basics about me, my family, and my friends. A few letters later, all we had in common was that our birthdays were two days apart. Even though I hadn't found the kindred spirit I had hoped for, we continued to write our awkward letters.

Not long after we began writing, Shan's family moved to a different state. From then on, the tone of our letters changed. Shan shared her feelings about the move, being away from friends, and adjusting to a new environment. Even though I wasn't sure what Shan was going through, I let her know she had a friend in me.

After that, Shan and I let down our guard and got rid of any inhibitions we had toward our friendship. Our letters turned into e-mails, and we wrote nearly every day. Over time we found we had more in common than we had at first thought. We both had older siblings, a passion for reading, the same taste in movies, and strong beliefs that we loved to defend! We both adored kids and shared baby-sitting tips and stories. Most of all, we both respected each other.

Our bond and friendship were soon tested again. Through my eighth- and ninth-grade years, my parents' marriage went downhill. The divorce devastated me. I tried to talk to other "divorced kids," but they didn't help. It was like divorce was "no big deal" to them. So I took a chance and talked to Shan about it. I thought that since she had a happy home life, she wouldn't understand what I was going through. I couldn't have been more wrong.

Shan sent me songs, gave me advice on handling my parents, and reassured me that this was not my fault. Most important, though, she listened. She didn't blow it off like most of my other friends. Without her friendship, I don't think I could have handled the divorce the way I did!

It's been almost six years since our first letter, and Shan and I still write twice a week. We share every little detail of our lives.

Shan and I aren't in the same town, so we don't have typical friendship problems. We aren't concerned about social circles, friends influencing the way we think of each other, or conflicting schedules. And we don't have to get to know each other quickly. By putting aside my inhibitions and being open-minded, I've found in Shan one of the best friends I know I will ever have.

Katie B.

Age 15, Virginia

Katie, left, and Shanna meet for the first time.

Friends for Life

Snail mail pal makes Shanna shine.

It's hard to describe the role Katie has played in my life. Who would have thought a pen pal could become the friend of a lifetime?

I have been homeschooled most of my life. Katie has been in public school. I have always taken my faith and religious beliefs very seriously, while Katie has just begun to get comfortable with hers. Katie is more outgoing, self-confident, and popular than I will ever be. And we have different plans for our futures. I want to be a stay-at-home mom, and Katie plans to pursue a career.

With all of our differences, I doubt if Katie and I would ever have become friends if we had both lived in the same town. Even if we had a connection, like through a class project, I don't think we would have taken the time to get to know each other.

I remember when I wanted Katie to be like me and told her so on a regular basis. Thankfully, I am past that. I truly accept Katie for the wonderful person she is, inside and out. So what makes Katie such a great friend? She puts up with my true colors, moods, and phases with understanding and loyalty.

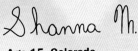

Age 15, Colorado

Just for Laughs

Rachel clowns around with comedy.

I started performing as a clown with my dad when I was eight, and I fell in love with clowning. I love the magic. Laughing makes me forget all the things that bug me. My cheeks hurt and my chest feels like it's about to burst. Then I relax. Laughter gives you the power to change yourself and people around you.

Rachel with her dad, Gershon, also known as "Buffo the Clown"

At one point in my life, I wasn't having a good time in school. I didn't like my teacher, and I'd lost confidence in academics and myself. One day my mom was reading a local paper and saw an ad for a writing class—or so she thought. It turned out to be a stand-up comedy workshop, and she asked me if I was interested. I said sure!

So on a Sunday afternoon I headed off to comedy class with a few jokes in hand. When it was my turn to take the mike, I started to shake and my knees knocked.

Since then, I've learned a lot about stand-up comedy. You tell stories. And you don't have to look much farther than my family to find funny stories. Some of my material is about being a clown's kid, so my dad is a huge resource. My mom isn't too shabby, either! She cracks unexpected jokes and has been known to do ridiculous dances anywhere, at any time. When my younger sister gets into a scrape, she makes up an outrageous story. It's so funny, she doesn't get into trouble. Living with this crowd, you have to be funny!

Sometimes when I perform, a joke will "bomb," and then I make a joke about "bombing." But the trick is to keep on with the performance even if no one laughs.

After about eight months of learning how to make people laugh, I was invited to do a real show in front of a real audience. I was so scared! I had five short bits that I kept going over and over in my mind.

Before I knew it, it was show time. The music blared and the lights dimmed. The emcee went onstage and did her material. She called on the first performer, the second, and then the third. As soon as she called my name, I froze! In a daze and on autopilot, I walked to the stage and lowered the microphone.

I was the youngest person and the only girl to perform. I looked out and could see only the people in the first row, because the lights blinded me. I was sure they could hear my heart pounding, while I stared at their french fries and drinks.

It seemed like an hour, but it was only seconds before I took a deep breath and said into the mike, "Wow, this is really scary. It just goes to show that my mom is right about one thing. I will do anything to get out of doing my homework!"

Rachel R.

Age 11, New York

Behind the Wheels

Corinne spends one day in a wheelchair.

Our school participated in a program where students could try life in a wheelchair for a day. My turn came on a Tuesday. To make the experience realistic, I had to stay in the wheelchair. I learned to pivot, push, direct, and brake the chair.

The worst part was the halls. It was unnerving that everyone was at least a foot taller and much more agile than I was. So many people were crammed into the halls that I frequently had to stop and start my chair so I wouldn't run into them. Students used my chair to steady themselves. Others pushed me along, steered me where they wanted me to go, or sent me careening into walls!

Our school is handicapped accessible, so most of my classes were easy to get to. But it was the simple things that turned out to be the most difficult, like getting behind and under a desk or maneuvering to get a drink of water. Paths grew tedious and my hands got sore.

The day after using the wheelchair, I realized how difficult it would be to live and work in one. I was glad to return the chair. I just wish that all handicapped people could turn in their wheelchairs at the end of the day, too.

Corinne W.

Age 14, Washington

The Girls' Club
Sarah learns more about Mom at a book club.

My mother and I have always had a good relationship, but as I got older and approached my teen years, it was sometimes more difficult to relate to her. One day I had an opportunity to change that.

Sarah and her mom, Chris, share similar reading tastes

The bookshop where I worked part-time asked me to head up a new project. I wasn't quite sure how Mom would respond.

"Mom, Ms. Elisabeth asked me if you and I would be interested in leading a mother/daughter book group," I said with uncertainty.

"Well, do you want to do it?" Mom asked. "It's entirely up to you."

I had never considered anything like this before. I thought the group might help me to understand my mom better, and I hoped that through this experience, she would come to understand me better as well. I decided to go with my gut feeling.

I was excited for the first official meeting of the Big and Little Women Book Group. And I was really nervous for five reasons:

1) I hoped somebody would show up.
2) I hoped the somebody who showed up enjoyed the book.
3) I hoped I didn't sound like a bumbling idiot.
4) I hoped my mother wouldn't do something embarrassing.
5) I hoped the brownies wouldn't melt on my new pants.

Soon the bookstore was packed. At first everyone was nervous, but as the meeting progressed, we couldn't stop talking. I was surprised at some of Mom's comments, and I actually agreed with many of them! I realized that Mom and I weren't that different after all. Because the discussion was a huge success, we planned to meet again.

Once the meeting was over, I wanted to talk with Mom. "Well, what did you think, Mom?" I asked.

"I really enjoyed it. You made some outstanding comments, real intellectual ones," Mom said, smiling. "So how do you think I did? Was I intellectual enough?"

"Yes, Mom," I said. "You were fantastic!"

Sarah J.

Age 13, Louisiana

Detectives on Duty
Johanna and her cousin solve a case.

Johanna and Elaine

My cousin Elaine and I started a detective agency. Our first big case came to us inside a plastic tube in a building filled with tubes and slides for kids. A voice behind us shouted, "Can you help me find my little brother?"

We were, as always, prepared with backpacks, cameras, notepads, pens, and magnifying glasses. Elaine and I were excited, but we followed rule #1: Stay calm. I asked the boy his brother's age, hair color, what he was wearing, and where we would meet after we found him. Then Elaine and I hurried off to solve The Case of the Missing Brother.

The boy's age was near Elaine's little sister's age. My younger cousin was playing in the balls. Might the lost boy be in the balls, too? Then we saw him—a blond boy wearing a blue shirt with a dragon on it, just as the brother had described.

Elaine and I had cracked our first case! It wasn't a complicated case, but it felt incredible! We are always ready for a good mystery.

Johanna M.
Age 12, Indiana

Nice Girl Finishes First

Brittany finds a bag packed with cash.

My mother, grandmother, and I were coming out of a shopping center when I saw a small bag on the ground in the parking lot. People were walking by and stepping all over it, but I picked it up.

I opened the bag and saw five $20 bills inside, then found a bank envelope with five $100 bills in it. That made $600 in all!

We immediately started to look for identification so we could return the money. We found receipts, makeup, and a copy of a driver's license. We had the lady's name, so we thought it would be easy to find her. It wasn't.

The first thing we did was put an ad in the local newspaper, but we didn't get a response. Finally, we called a number on one of the receipts. It was a car dealership. The man said that he knew the woman we were looking for and that she should be in any day to make a car payment. We asked him to give her our phone number.

A week later, the lady's daughter called us. They were Mexican and her mother didn't speak English, but the daughter described exactly what was in the bag.

We decided to meet the woman and her daughter in the same parking lot where I found the bag. When I returned the bag, the woman was very happy. She gave me a big hug and wanted to give me a $40 reward. I didn't need a reward, but she wanted to show her appreciation, so I accepted $20. I felt glad we were able to return her money. It was close to Christmas, and I imagined that she would need the money to buy gifts for her kids.

When I told friends about the money, some of them said, "I would keep the money," or "Do you know how much stuff $600 can buy?" I asked them if they had lost $600, would they have wanted it back?

My grandmother told me that if I do the right things in life, good things will happen to me. She was right! After I returned the money, I won a beauty pageant and made dance line at my school.

Doing something good for someone else makes you happier on the inside than anything else ever could. But don't take my word for it. Do something nice for someone today and see for yourself.

Brittany T.

Age 12, Alabama

Girl proves honesty remains a virtue

If you're feeling down about human nature, this story of a you...

All Choked Up

Jessenia fights for her life.

What started as a game of handball in front of my home ended as one of the scariest moments of my life.

I was sucking on a jawbreaker, and I'd moved it from one side of my mouth to the other when it accidentally slipped down my throat. Suddenly, I couldn't breathe. I was suffocating, and I panicked. I couldn't talk! How could I let my friends know I was choking? All I could do was point to my throat.

Would they understand? How long could I stand here and not breathe? Was I going to die? All of these thoughts raced through my mind. I felt desperate with no air in my lungs. I knew my face was turning red, because I started to feel hot. I still had no air!

I could see friends racing into the house for help. I felt so scared, so alone. But then I saw Francesca was still with me. I could feel her arms squeezing my stomach. Then, inside my stomach, I felt a huge gush of air force the jawbreaker out of my throat and onto the ground. It felt good as I sucked deeply, inhaling wonderful air. I was so relieved to finally breathe again. I hugged Francesca and thanked her for saving my life.

I will always remember what happened. Francesca didn't leave. She didn't panic. She just stayed and saved my life. She will always be a special person to me.

Jessenia L.

Age 11, California

Calm, Cool, and Clever
A cartoon helps Francesca save a friend's life.

I could immediately tell something was wrong with Jessenia. Her eyes were wide open, and by the look on her face, I could tell she was really scared and unable to breathe.

While most of our friends ran inside to get help, I felt I needed to stay with Jessenia. I could feel a guardian angel next to me. She said, "It's O.K. Stay calm. You're going to help your friend."

Suddenly, I remembered a cartoon that shows a character doing the Heimlich maneuver on a choking victim! I ran behind Jessenia and wrapped my arms around her. It was hard. I'd never done the Heimlich before! Would it work? Were my hands in the right place? I didn't want to push her stomach in hard at first, because I didn't want to hurt her.

After three light thrusts, the jawbreaker was still stuck. I could tell Jessenia was really panicked now. She turned around and again pointed at her throat. I swung her back around and pushed on her stomach harder. I had to try again. My friend's life depended on it. If I didn't, I could lose my friend.

And then I saw the jawbreaker on the ground in front of us.

It hit me why it's important to stay calm in a scary situation. If you panic, you can't move or think, and that makes the situation worse. You need to help that person—maybe save that person's life.

Francesca V.

Age 10, California

45

Puppy Love

Breanna comforts a hurt dog.

One night I was sitting on the couch watching television. My dad had just stepped outside when he heard a splash. He ran toward the river and saw a dog in the water. My father called the police.

Once the police arrived, they pulled the dog out of the cold water. As soon as I learned what had happened, I put on my shoes, grabbed my canes, and ran outside as fast as I could.

My father let me see the dog. He was beautiful. I wanted to pet him so badly, but my dad wanted me to wait to see how the dog would react to me first.

In spite of my father's advice, I snuck over to the dog. He kept trying to come to me and I didn't want the dog to hurt himself even more. I sat on the ground, cuddled him, and told him things to calm him down.  I knew what to say. I had had 15 surgeries already. I have a disease that causes dwarfism, brittle bones, and arthritis. So I understood his pain. I knew not to move him too much. Surprisingly, he wasn't scared of me and didn't even growl. Instead, the dog started to cuddle back!

I could tell his leg hurt badly. I knew what that felt like, since I use canes to help me walk. So I wrapped him in a blanket to keep him warm, talked to him to calm him down, and even gave him a temporary name: Cutie.

The police took hours to find a vet to examine Cutie. The vet discovered the dog had a fractured leg, but said he would survive, even though he had gone off a 30-foot bridge.

After the veterinarian had finished with Cutie, we took him to the Humane Society, where he would stay until he was adopted. I didn't want Cutie to live with another family. I wanted him to live with me. I bugged my parents about adopting the dog for days.

Later that week, my parents picked me up from school and took me to adopt Cutie! After we brought him home, we changed his name to Survivor. I wouldn't give Survivor up for anything. I have gotten closer to him than I could have ever imagined. He has shown me how much just a little love can change a person.

Breanna O.

Age 11, New York

Both Breanna and Survivor are happy about how this story turned out!

Bus Stop!

Shannon helps stop a runaway bus.

It started off as a normal morning. I got on the bus, said hi to Nick, the bus driver, and then I sat down in my usual spot, the second seat across the aisle from Nick.

Things changed about a mile from school. I realized something was wrong. The school bus was veering off to the side of the road! I looked up at Nick and was shocked to see him fainting on top of the steering wheel.

My first thought was that he was having a heart attack, so I knew that I needed to get help right away. I stood up and yelled, "Nick is having a heart attack!" Some of the kids thought I was joking, but they immediately saw I wasn't kidding around.

I was afraid to take the steering wheel by myself, so I asked Matt to help. Nick was passed out, slumped over the wheel. We had to lift him up just so Matt could steer.

Two other boys got up to help control the bus. By now, many of the kids were scared, including me. My biggest fear was that everyone would get out of control and the bus would be left out in the middle of the street to be hit by another car. I knew we had to look out for ourselves or something bad was going to happen.

Then I felt incredibly peaceful. Something inside me knew not to panic. I remembered my mom had prayed for me before I left for school, so I felt we were in good hands.

I suddenly remembered the bus safety training I'd had in elementary school. The first thing they taught us was to stay calm in scary situations. So as calmly as I could, I told everyone to sit down. I said that the situation was under control— and we got the bus stopped.

Today Nick is fine. It turns out that he didn't faint from a heart attack but from the flu. After he got better, he was back driving our bus!

Our school bus adventure was the talk of the town for a few days. We were on the front page of a big city newspaper. We had radio and television interviews. The school board and city representatives presented us with a certificate of achievement. They called us heroes. If being a hero means staying calm in a scary situation, then I guess we were.

Shannon S.

Age 12, Minnesota

Trash to Treasure

Jeni rescues a drowning kitten.

Last year my friend Valerie and I were at the lake with our families. We were watching boats go by when we saw a man throw a small object from his boat into the water. I thought it was garbage, so we went out to pick it up.

You can imagine our surprise when we saw that it wasn't trash at all, but a baby kitten! She could barely keep her head above water and was crying so loudly, it hurt my ears!

Valerie jumped into the lake and rescued the kitten, and then we rushed back to shore. We gave a description of the man to the news, and they reported it, but we haven't heard anything yet.

We didn't think the kitten would live. She was wet and shivering. We dried her off, trying to rub warmth back into her. A clerk at the pet store said our kitten was only a few weeks old. Her eyes weren't completely open yet, and she fit right in the palm of my hand. We had to feed her a special formula with an eyedropper until she was old enough to eat on her own.

My cousin adopted the kitten and named her 'Lucky Jo.' Now she is a happy, funny cat and seems to know that she is a lucky one!

Jeni S.

Age 14, Washington

A Call for Help

A plea leaves Mikayla stuck for hours.

One day I was home flipping through the channels on my walkie-talkie. Not much was coming in. Then I heard someone say, "Is anyone out there?"

It was a man calling on his walkie-talkie for help! He was hiking with friends and had sprained his ankle. Usually my walkie-talkie only picks up radio signals within two miles, but this man was on a mountain 100 miles away!

I told my mom what was happening and took the walkie-talkie outside so I could hear the man better. I couldn't move more than a foot away or I'd lose touch with him.

 Mom called the sheriff, who arranged for a helicopter. The sheriff had me ask the man to describe where he was, and then the sheriff told the pilot. I stayed in the same spot for more than four hours talking to the injured man. The helicopter had a hard time landing because the area was rocky, but the pilot did rescue him.

Later, I got to meet the man who was hurt. He was surprised I was so young. Now, my family always takes our walkie-talkie when we go camping—just in case we need to call for help!

Mikayla W.

Age 11, Washington

51

Monkey Business

Ellen goes ape over rescuing chimps.

 I got a gift from my fantastic grandparents that changed my life. It was a book about Jane Goodall, the woman famous for rescuing chimpanzees. After reading it, I fell in love with the animals.

As I got older, my mom and I started a Roots and Shoots club at my school, determined to rescue chimpanzees just like Jane.

Our first mission was to raise money to pay for the chimps' care in sanctuaries in Africa. Sanctuaries are safe places for chimps who can no longer live on their own in natural habitats because of deforestation or poaching. We sold 600 chocolate bars—enough to save five chimps!

Sponsoring chimps means a lot to me. I've learned their worst enemy is the poacher. These people kill chimps for meat or body parts. They will even kill baby chimps' parents so they can sell the babies for commercials, movies, circuses, or pets!

Maybe in the future, people will respect animals in the wild. Until then, we need to do what we can to help.

Ellen J.

Age 10, Pennsylvania

To find out more about chimps, go to *janegoodall.org*.

the Jane Goodall Institute
CHIMPANZEE GUARDIAN PROGRAM

Tired of Teasing

Jennifer stands up to bullies.

I must have seemed like an easy target. When I started middle school, kids started to tease me. They teased me for little things, like the way I walked, talked, or laughed. At one point, a girl on the school bus smeared mascara on my glasses.

All the teasing and harassment made me sad and angry. I would often go home in tears. There were even days I didn't want to go to school, let alone ride the bus, because I was afraid of the teasing that awaited me.

My mother said she didn't want to take me to school and pick me up for the next three years, so she suggested I talk with a school counselor. I did and discovered that I wasn't alone. Lots of kids were getting teased—even some of my best friends!

After months of torment, my friends and I finally decided that enough was enough! We wrote a petition to the principal describing what we saw going on in class and in the halls.

With the principal's support, we organized a group of students who had been teased. Our goal as a group was to reduce and prevent teasing in our school. It took us almost a whole school year of hard work to put together a program.

We gave our anti-bully presentation to every sixth-grade class and some fifth-grade classes as well. None of us, including myself, thought the program would be successful. But we figured that if we could help at least one or two people, we would be doing well.

To our amazement, the program worked! Teachers said that they noticed a lot less teasing and bullying.

If you are being teased, you aren't alone. Everyone, no matter how popular, gets teased at least a little bit. Just remember that there is always someone to go to for support—a close friend, a parent, a relative, or another adult. The anti-bullying program changed my life. If bullying is a problem at your school, maybe you and your classmates can help make a difference, too.

Jennifer M.

Age 14, Indiana

Jennifer (kneeling, holding the plaque) and her "Making School Better" committee were given a "Character Counts" award by the mayor of their city.

A Special Song

Savannah uses poetry to overcome pain.

Gage, our golden retriever, and I did many things together. We played catch and tug-of-war. He let me lay my head on him when I watched television or took naps. And when I was smaller, I would even ride him like a horse!

Savannah with Gage

One day Gage didn't feel well. He stopped eating and acted tired. We took him to our veterinarian. The next day the vet called and told us that my Gage was very sick. His kidneys weren't working anymore. Gage had Lyme disease. The vet kept him all weekend to try to make him better.

That Monday, my parents came to pick me up early. I was excited because that was the day Gage was supposed to come home. I thought he was all better and good as new.

When my brother and I got in the car, my mom and dad told us that we needed to tell Gage that we loved him. What my dad was telling us was to say good-bye. Suddenly, my legs felt like jelly and my heart started to beat really fast. I began to cry.

When we arrived at the vet's office, Gage wagged his tail so wildly, I thought it was going to fly off his body. But he was still very tired and couldn't get up. I hugged him tightly and kissed his nose and ears and cheek. I sang him a song called "You Are My Sunshine," even though I didn't know all the words. Then the vet gave him a needle and he went to sleep forever. Gage was only three years old when he died, and it was the saddest day of my entire life.

The next night we buried Gage under his favorite shade tree. My mom told me that when I missed him, I should look up in the sky and find the biggest, fluffiest, and furriest star and I would see Gage.

One day after school, my mom asked me about my poem book. I told her I wrote poems to Gage to help him and me feel better. My dad plays guitar and he started to sing one of my poems to me!

It sounded so good, I asked Dad if I could create a compact disc using my poems and his music. I wrote to the Humane Society and told them I wanted to donate any earnings from my CD to educate people about Lyme disease. The people there were very excited about my plan.

So far my CD called "I See You in the Stars at Night" has raised about $1,000 for Lyme disease awareness.

A year after Gage died, my mom and dad gave my brother and me a golden retriever puppy. We named him Buccaneer Gage. I think he was sent to me from heaven because he's just what I needed to feel good again. I think Gage sent him to me. He is telling me that it's O.K. to love Buccaneer.

Savannah W.

Age 9, Maryland

Lemonade for You

Julia squeezes hope from a lemonade stand.

My cousin, Jonathan Neff Cappello, age 23, worked at the World Trade Center. He was a bond trader for Cantor Fitzgerald on the 105th floor. That turned out to be the floor that got hit by a terrorist plane on September 11, 2001. Almost every person in Jonathan's company died.

Julia's cousin, Jonathan

Jonathan was nicknamed Jono for all of the mischief (Jon, no!) he got into as a child. He and I had a special bond. I was given his Cabbage Patch doll when I was a baby. The doll's name is Alfie, and I have slept with him almost every night of my life. For years I looked forward to visiting Jono, but, unfortunately, every time we went to New York, he was away at college. Then his recent plans to visit us fell through. When I heard about the terrorist attack, I knew it wouldn't be possible to ever see him again.

Deep down, I knew Jono wasn't coming out of that building. But I didn't know how to react. How should I have acted? That's not something somebody teaches you.

My family went to church that night and prayed for the phone call that never came—the one saying Jono was alive. By the next day, hope turned to anger and sadness. I did not want to go to school, play, or even talk to friends.

Tired of feeling helpless, sad, and angry, I decided to take action. My friend Caroline and I started a lemonade stand to raise money for the Red Cross in honor of Jono. My brother, neighbors, and friends helped at our stand. On the first day, we made $300. The second day we were up to $1,000. By our third day, we had raised $8,500. People were giving money without even taking lemonade. Because of the lemonade stand, I got a lot of publicity, but that was not the point. I started to feel better, and I knew that Jono was proud of me.

I am now back to my usual chatterbox self and active in soccer and gymnastics—things I had taken a break from because of worrying that bad things could happen. After raising money for September 11 victims, I quit worrying all the time. I think it is because I put my energy into helping other people. I made something tragic into something positive.

Julia D.

Age 10, North Carolina

Sink or Swim

After a serious injury, Amanda learns to adapt.

I've loved swimming my whole life. I joined a swim team when I was in kindergarten. That's when I began racing competitively. I don't mean to brag, but I was a good swimmer.

I've also loved horses. I was taking riding lessons when my accident happened. I was to walk the horse down to the end of the arena, touch a bar, and then start my cool-off walk. I touched the bar and kicked my horse to start walking, but instead of walking, she took off galloping! The instructors hadn't yet taught me what to do if a horse started running, so I just held on for dear life. I'm not sure what happened after I fell off the horse. My brain blocked me from remembering. I woke up in the car thinking I had broken my arm.

The doctors told me my right arm was paralyzed. I don't remember them telling me that, but they must have.

After I got home, I quickly began to see how difficult my life would be now. Doing the things I loved, like writing, would be a challenge. You use two hands to write with: one to hold the paper and one to write.

And I didn't think I would be able to compete in swimming meets again. My sister and most of my friends were still on the team, but I couldn't go watch. It was too depressing. That was the worst summer of my life.

The next year, I was tired of being left out of something that I loved and was good at. I was determined to be on the swim team—and to win my races! My swim therapist, Ingrid, gave me confidence in my ability to compete. And my coach, Laura Lynn, along with my team, supported and encouraged me.

Before long, I was swimming, having tons of fun, and winning my races. I even nabbed a fourth place in the championships for backstroke! And I still enjoy horseback riding, but now I ride at a ranch that specializes in helping children overcome problems or disabilities.

The pain in my hand and the pain of being left out were terrible, but I overcame them. I've learned a lot about myself: I am determined. I don't like people to treat me like I'm different. And I'm more patient than I ever thought I would be.

I can't go back in time and fix things, or I would. So I've learned to accept and adapt to things that happen. These days, I don't let anyone tell me I can't do something. If they say I can't, I do it! It just feels good to prove them wrong.

Amanda E.

Age 12, Kansas

Tough Times

Michelle makes it through the pain of loss.

It's funny how life works. You can be thrust from childhood to adulthood in a matter of seconds. This is the story of how life threw me for a loop.

More than a year ago, my dad took my younger brother Sam and me to the park. (I hold my breath whenever I pass that park now.) He sat us down and, with tears in his eyes, told us that our mom wasn't going to live much longer than a week.

My mom had been diagnosed with cancer when I was nine. Surgery was successful, so she began chemotherapy to eradicate the disease. Unfortunately, four years later, the cancer returned. More surgeries, more medicine, and this time, more tumors. Complications arose, and we found ourselves camping out in the unit of the hospital where they don't send you home.

Michelle with her mom

That brings me back to the park. I had known all along my mom wasn't going to make it, but hearing it was tough. We went back to the hospital, but I couldn't talk and could barely even look at my own mother. That was the last time I got to see her. My mom died on February 15, the day after Valentine's Day.

My aunt and grandmother took my brother and me to get something to wear for the funeral. I chose a bright red shirt and flowery skirt. I was willing to do anything to keep busy. Adrenaline constantly ran through my body, trying to stop me from losing my mind.

Eventually, everyone left and things started to quiet down. Quiet is where the trouble starts. Quiet gives you time to think. People asked me if it was nice getting back to normal. What, normal? What's normal about a 14-year-old girl not having a mom? I always said I was fine, even put on a smile. Then the quiet would come back, always at night, always alone.

I started seeing a psychologist. At first I talked about nonsense stuff, like the weather or why my brother insisted on wearing the same shirt for a week. Then the heavy stuff came—questions like why did my mom have to die and why did I feel such conflicting emotions.

But one day, things became clearer. And suddenly, I realized that over time, I had been able to deal with my mom's death by myself. My anguish was slowly fading away.

I still go to my psychologist, talking this time about boys, friends, and anything else going on in my life. I have become a stronger and wiser person. Life can get hard, but you can overcome the tough times and move on. That doesn't mean forgetting what you have overcome— just making the best of things.

Michelle B.

Age 15, North Carolina

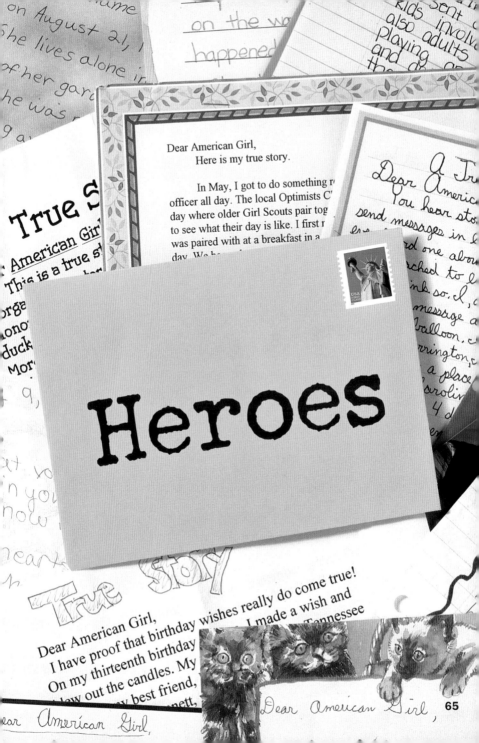

Minnie and the Moose

Tanya's best friend saves her life.

My best friend in the whole wide world is a dog named Minnie. She's an Alaskan malamute, and she saved my life.

I was in Alaska and was helping my two younger cousins, Alyeska and Elan, build a snow fort. All of a sudden, Minnie started to growl. I looked up and couldn't believe my eyes. Right in front of us stood a moose!

I knew that a moose could stomp on us and really hurt us. But then things got worse. I heard rustling behind me. Out from the trees came the moose's babies. They were standing right behind us—and we were stuck in the middle.

In an instant, the moose started to charge at us. Boy, was I scared! I realized I couldn't run in the knee-deep snow without falling. It was like my feet were stuck in cement. Even so, I felt responsible for getting my four- and six-year-old cousins inside safely. I just wasn't sure how to do it.

Then Minnie did something amazing. She jumped on the moose and bit into its neck! Minnie kept the moose  distracted just long enough to let me round up the girls and get them inside. Once we were inside, Minnie followed after us.

My moose encounter taught me two valuable lessons: First, never get stuck between a moose and her babies. And second, a good friend will always stick up for you—even if she is a dog.

Tanya C.
Age 10, Pennsylvania

Tanya with her hero, Minnie

Running Home
Caroline swings into action for a friend.

I had a friend named Emily Derer. She was an amazing, kind, and loving person. Unfortunately, she died in her sleep. All of my friends and I were heartbroken.

Emily was a member of our softball team. When she was playing, she always tried her hardest. Emily had a noncancerous brain tumor. It affected one of her legs, so she had to wear a brace. This made it very difficult for her to run the bases. Most of the time she would strike out, but once in a while, she'd get to first base. One day, she made it all the way to home base! She was so happy.

All for one! Front row: Chelsea, Colleen, Kristin, Caroline, Michelle, Emily; back row: Jim, Heather, Sarah B., Kayla, Katie, Haley, Karen, and Belle; not pictured: Amanda, Sarah N., Kelsey, Melissa, Barb, Steve

After Emily died, Kelsey, Sarah, Melissa, Kristin, Colleen, and I wanted to do something in memory of her. Because Emily loved softball, we thought it would be a good idea to name a softball diamond after her.

It wasn't easy. My friends, coaches, and I had to talk to the city parks board, whose members unanimously agreed to name the diamond after Emily. Then we had to talk to the city council. At first they wanted to shut down our proposal. They said our plan wasn't possible because there were no rules about naming buildings, parks, or fields in our city.

But we kept at it. During the school's announcements, we told everyone about the petition for the diamond. More than 600 people signed it! We also got support from parents, teachers, classmates—even most of the city council! We did what Emily would have done. We didn't give up.

One woman disagreed, but she gave in by the second meeting. After we finally had approval to go ahead, we had to raise $200 for a sign, have a company make us a sign, then get together to paint the sign so that it would look like other signs in our city. Before long, we had a dedication ceremony for the opening of the "Emily Derer Diamond." That night, Emily's father threw out the first ball.

We did all of this because softball meant a lot to Emily. We felt that this was the best way to remember her. I know that she would think having a softball diamond named after her was awesome.

From now on, playing at the diamond will be special. When I pass by home plate, I think Emily will be there with me, glad to have made it home one more time.

Caroline H.
Age 14, Wisconsin

Emily Derer Diamond

My Mr. Nice Man

Chantyl remembers a hero.

I would not be here to tell you this story if it were not for a man who, to me, is the best hero who ever lived.

It all started when I was three years old and my parents found out that I had a deadly disease called aplastic anemia. The only cure was a bone marrow transplant. The doctors put me on a registry for a donor since no one in my family was a match. In the meantime, I developed a cancer called T-cell lymphoma. My chances of survival were slim.

When I was five years old, I got my transplant from "My Mr. Nice Man." That's what I called him because I was not allowed to know his name for one full year after my transplant had taken place. As soon as a year passed from my very successful transplant, I learned that the real name of "My Mr. Nice Man" was Terry. He lived in New York and was also a hero in many other people's lives. Terry was a New York firefighter.

I met Terry and his family in person a year after my transplant. I knew as soon as I met him that I would love him as long as I lived. Every breath that I take is because of him. And every drop of my blood that flows through my veins is his blood, too.

After another five years had passed from our first meeting, I traveled back to New York to surprise Terry. I wanted him to see how well I was doing and how much I had grown. I also wanted to thank him again in person. I didn't think I could ever tell him that enough. I had plans to visit Terry every five years throughout my life.

Sadly, my hopes went up in smoke on September 11, 2001. Terry lost his own life at the World Trade Center. He rushed into the building that was attacked by terrorists. The World Trade Center collapsed, killing thousands of people, including Terry. But Terry died doing what he did best—saving lives.

Today I am a very healthy and active 13-year-old girl who owes everything to My Mr. Nice Man . . . Terry.

For Terry: I love you and pray for you and your family every day, and I know that someday we will all be together again. I will live the rest of my life trying to do my best so that you can continue to be proud of me and proud that you saved my life.

Chantyl P.

Age 13, Nevada

Chantyl always keeps a place for Terry on her mantel at home.

My True Story
Dear Editor: I have a story to tell.

If we use your story in an American Girl book or magazine, we will
contact you first. Send your name, phone number, and birth date to:

True Stories Book Editor
American Girl Library
8400 Fairway Place
Middleton, Wisconsin 53562